THE PUFFINS ARE BACK!
NEW AND UPDATED

BY GAIL GIBBONS

HOLIDAY HOUSE
NEW YORK

Special thanks to Stephen Kress, research biologist
at the National Audobon Society, and Paul Sweet,
ornithologist at the American Museum of Natural History.

The artwork for *The Puffins Are Back!* was done on
140 pound Arches watercolor paper, using a
combination of watercolors, colored pencils, and
black ink.

The Library of Congress has cataloged the prior edition as follows:
Gibbons, Gail.
The puffins are back! / Gail Gibbons
p. cm.
Summary: A simple introduction to the physical
characteristics, life cycle, and natural environment
of the puffins living off the coast of Maine.
ISBN 0-06-021603-4.—ISBN 0-06-021604-2 (lib. bdg.)
1. Atlantic puffin—Juvenile literature. [1. Puffins.] I. Title.
QL696.C42G53   1991   90-30525
598'.33–dc20   CIP   AC

ISBN 978-0-8234-4163-1 (hardcover)

A small boat comes close to an island off the coast of Maine. A gentle wave pushes it ashore. A group of people steps onto the rocky beach.

These scientists are from the National Audubon Society, an organization involved in the study and protection of wildlife—especially birds.

They have come to study a puffin colony. A different team will come to the island every two weeks throughout the spring and summer. Atlantic puffins are seabirds that leave the water only to lay their eggs and raise their young. Each year in the spring, most puffins return to the places where they were hatched, rugged shores on isolated islands.

Scientists have learned that puffins return to their birthplace as if they are on a schedule.

This year the puffins off the coast of Maine are right on time! They have come back on the same day as they did last year, at almost exactly the same hour.

Over the next few days, the puffins gather in large groups, or "rafts," offshore.

During most of the year, puffins are not very colorful. But every spring, a horny coloring grows on puffins' bills, and their three-toed, webbed feet become bright orange. These splashes of orange and yellow give the puffins a comical look. Some people have named them "clowns of the sea" or "sea parrots."

The puffins bob up and down on the waves. They are excellent swimmers and divers. When they dive underwater to catch fish, their wings beat against the water in a movement similar to a bird flying. Layers of fat and thick, dense feathers insulate them from the cold water.

A puffin has two sets of eyelids, inner and outer. These inner lids shield the puffin's eyes from seawater while it darts about, hunting for food.

Every year at this time the puffins begin to pair off, each one finding its own mate. Usually, puffins mate and raise their young in the same pairs, year after year. The males and females look very much alike to us, but puffins seem to have no trouble recognizing their mates.

Meanwhile, on the island, the scientists are observing the puffins. They watch them through binoculars, taking careful notes.

For the next few days, the puffins chase one another playfully, rubbing and clapping their bills together.

The scientists know the puffins will soon come ashore. Sometimes they will need to study the puffins from inside a "blind." Blinds are shelters that keep the scientists hidden so they can watch the puffins up close without disturbing them.

All at once, the puffins rise from the surface of the sea. They fill the sky over the island and then come to the ground. Amazingly, although they spend most of the year out at sea, the puffins land on the island without too much trouble.

The scientists are glad to see so many puffins returning to the island!

In 1969, when scientists from the Audubon Society first started studying the puffins of Maine, they found very few. Ever since colonial days, puffins had been hunted for their feathers and their meat. Many, many birds were killed.

The scientists were worried that soon there would be no more puffins off the coast of Maine. They were concerned that the puffins would not survive without help, so the scientists worked out a plan.

They built burrows, almost like the ones puffins make for their young. Then the scientists brought newly hatched Atlantic puffin chicks to Maine from an island near Newfoundland. Many puffins still gathered there to mate and lay their eggs.

The scientists put a band on each chick's leg. This would help to identify the puffins that came from Newfoundland and grew up in the man-made burrows. The scientists hoped that these chicks would remember Maine as their birthplace, and that they would return to Maine when they were ready to mate.

Then the scientists carefully placed a chick in each burrow. Since the chicks had been taken from their parents, the scientists fed them until they were ready to leave their nests.

It would take years before the scientists knew that their plan to help the puffins had worked.

Now, many years later, a scientific team continues to observe the puffins and take notes. The information the scientists gather during their stay on the island will be studied carefully during the coming year.

About two to three weeks after coming ashore, the female puffins will be ready to lay their eggs. Puffins don't build nests in trees like most other birds. Instead, they make burrows by picking at the ground with their sharp beaks and pushing the loosened dirt outward with their broad, webbed feet. Sometimes they clean out old burrows and use them over again, and often they build them under boulders. They build a small nest inside the burrow.

Each pair of adult puffins has its own territory and burrow. The male guards the female during nesting time. He will drive away any other bird that tries to invade their territory.

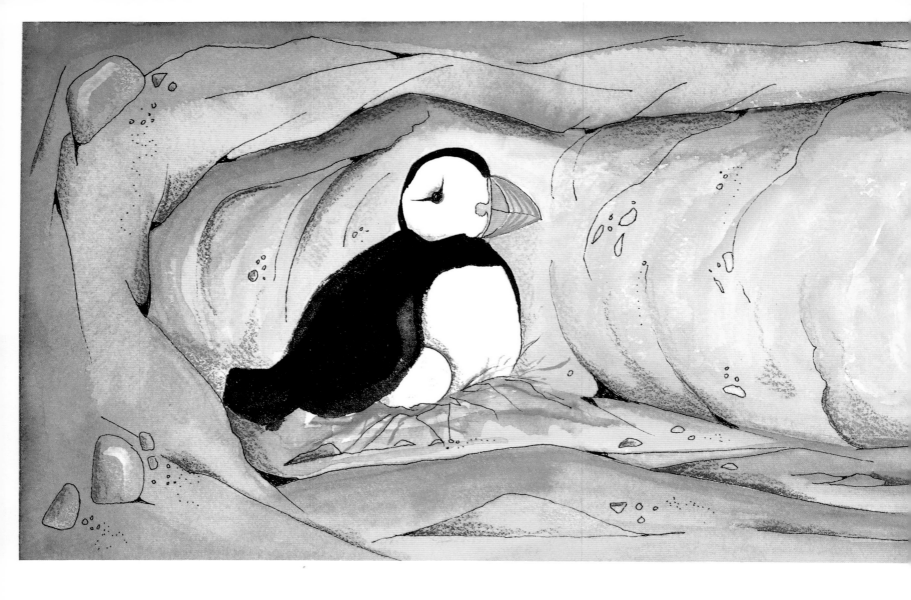

In early May, the female puffin lays one large egg. During the next forty days or so, both puffins take turns keeping the egg warm, incubating it. Most birds sit on their eggs. Puffins don't. Instead, the puffin tucks the egg under one wing and leans against it.

When they switch places on the nest, the puffins raise their heads and nuzzle their bills together. While one puffin keeps the egg warm, the other one guards the burrow entrance or makes short trips to bring back food.

The scientists have been keeping a careful count since the puffins arrived. There are many more puffins on the island than last year!

Two of the scientists use a telescope to take a closer look at one of the puffins. The puffin has a band on its leg, with a number. It was one of the puffin chicks that was brought from Newfoundland. It is an adult now and has returned to Maine to have its own young. Puffins can live to be almost forty years old. Most are ready to mate by the time they are four or five.

The scientists carefully record the puffin's number. This puffin proves that the plan to restore the puffin population on the island is working. If more and more puffins continue to come back each year, the population of the puffin colony will increase.

The puffins have a good chance of surviving. The island has been declared a bird sanctuary—a protected place where the puffins will be left alone and where no hunting is allowed.

More than a month goes by. Finally, in one of the burrows, sound comes from an unhatched egg. The adult puffins respond with soft, soothing calls. Inside the shell, the puffin chick listens. Hearing its parents' calls over and over, the chick learns to recognize them. From the moment it is hatched, the puffin will know its parents by their calls.

Chip. Chip. Chip! The puffin chick pecks its way out of its shell. Puffins hatch with a fluffy coat of down feathers. Their eyes are open, and they can see.

Young puffins have big appetites. For the next six weeks, the parent puffins make many trips from the sea with their bills full of small herring, sand lance, and other fish. Some chicks in the puffinry, or nesting area, eat as many as two thousand fish during this time!

Click. One of the scientists takes a picture of an adult puffin waddling toward a burrow with its beak full of fish. A gull swoops down and steals a fish right out of the puffin's mouth.

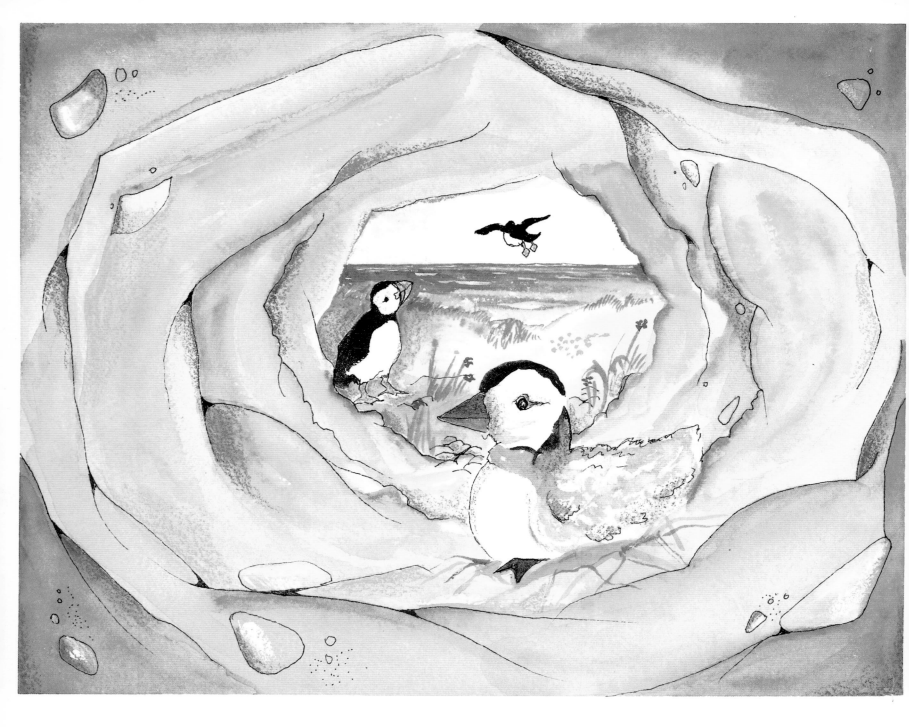

After six weeks of caring for their young, the parent puffins begin to lose their bright, clown-like colors. They are ready to take off from the island. They fly away to sea, leaving the chicks behind.

The young puffins stay safely nestled in their burrows. The chicks have been well fed. They can live off their body fat for about a week before getting hungry.

Click. Another picture. The scientists take snapshots of each other banding this year's chicks.

The puffins are seven weeks old now. The scientists have been watching them very carefully. They know the chicks will not stay in the burrows much longer.

Finally, they see a puffin chick leaving its burrow for the first time. One by one, the other young puffins stroll out of their burrows, too.

The chicks come out at night, when gulls, their natural enemies, are asleep. They head directly toward the shore. Trying to fly, they make a leap. The puffins tumble into the moonlit waters with a splash. They have reached the sea, and they feel right at home there.

The puffins begin to swim, to dive, and to catch food.

The scientists onshore watch them drift away from the island. The job of observing and banding the puffins is over until next year.

The young puffins will be on their own now, facing the dangers of the open sea. They will not return to the island for two or three years. But the adult puffins will be back next spring, and so will the scientists who watch them.

A NOTE FROM THE AUTHOR

In the summer, my husband and I live on Matinicus Island off the coast of Maine. From our house, we look at an island called Matinicus Rock, which is six miles away. A colony of puffins nest and raise their young on the island each year. —G. G.

Tourists are not allowed to be on the islands where the puffins are nesting. Only the scientists from the Puffin Project, and other trained people, may visit and study the puffins.

Atlantic puffins mate, nest, and raise their young between April 1 and August 31.

Some people pay to take boats near islands such as Eastern Egg Rock, off the coast of Maine, so they can watch the puffins.

Atlantic puffins always return to the islands they were born on to mate and raise their young.

The National Audubon Society's Puffin Project is a total success. Atlantic puffin colonies are flourishing on a number of islands off the coast of Maine, especially Eastern Egg Rock and Matinicus Rock.

Atlantic puffins can dive about 200 feet (60 m) underwater in search of food, though most of their dives are shallower.

60% of Atlantic puffins nest and breed on Icelandic islands.

Atlantic puffins are about 10 inches (18 cm) tall.

Puffins spend most of their lives out at sea, resting on the waves, or "rafting," when not swimming.